THE WAY IT WAS
THE WAY IT WAS
THE WAY IT WAS

The Vikings in Scotland

Stories from the sagas

ERIC SIMPSON

SERIES EDITOR: BRIAN CHAPLIN

CHAMBERS

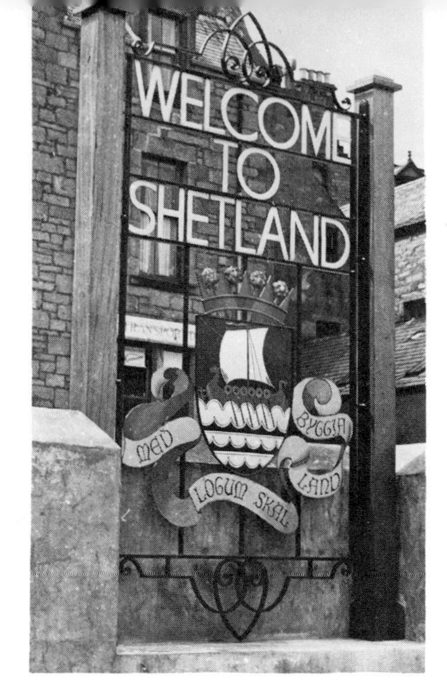

1. The Northern Isles

Here is a badge with a Viking ship on it. It is the coat of arms of Shetland, which, as you can see from the map, is the most northerly group of islands in Britain. The Shetland group are sometimes known as the Viking islands, because, like the neighbouring isles of Orkney, they were once ruled by the Vikings or Norsemen.

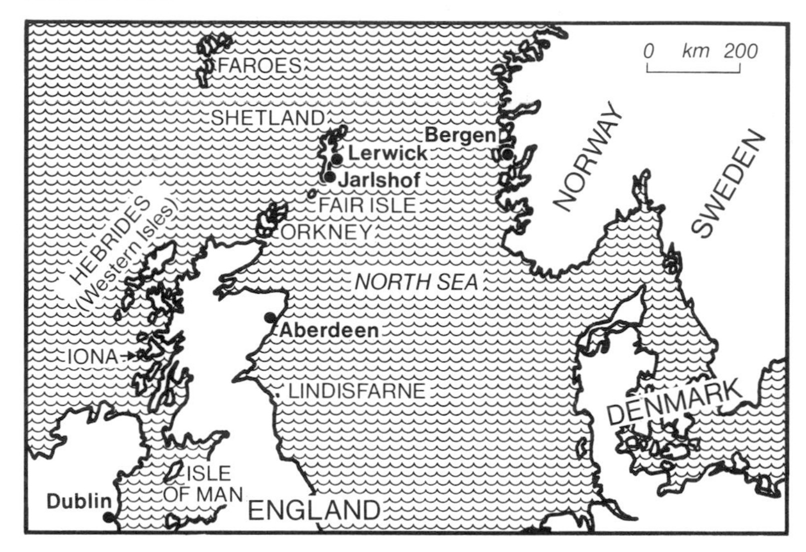

Historians do not know for sure when the Vikings first came to the Northern Isles (Orkney and Shetland), but they think that it was about 800. It was around this time that the Vikings, fierce Scandinavian raiders, made their first attacks on Britain, raiding lonely island monasteries like Lindisfarne and Iona. Unlike the warriors who attacked Lindisfarne and Iona, the Vikings who landed in Shetland and Orkney were settlers. These Norsemen, who had come from Norway, meant to stay. In later years many others were to settle in Britain, Norsemen in the Northern Isles and elsewhere in Scotland, Danes in southern Britain.

Although it is now hundreds of years since the Norse ceased to rule over Orkney and Shetland, even today there are many links with those far-off days, as you can see from the photographs in this chapter. Look again at the coat of arms. Can you see the motto below the badge? It is written in Old Norse, the ancient language of the Vikings. The motto, which comes from one of the Viking sagas, means: 'By the law shall the land be built up'.

To think about

1 *How can you tell that the people of Orkney and Shetland are proud of their Norse origins?*

2 *Find Shetland on the map on this page. If you lived in the north of Shetland, which would be nearer to you—Bergen in Norway or Aberdeen on the Scottish mainland?*

To find out

3 *Find the meaning of words like* saga, longship *and* sea-king. *Make a list of new words and their meanings. You can add to your list as you go through this book.*

4 *Find out the meaning of some of the place-names in your locality. Are any of them Norse?*

To do

5 *Draw a picture of, or write a poem about, the burning of the longship at the Up-Helly-A' festival.*

Look at this photograph of Lerwick, which is the capital of Shetland. In the harbour there are small sailing boats, which in their design resemble the much larger longships used by the Viking raiders. Compare the boats shown here with the Viking ship in the picture on page 5.

There are many other reminders of the days of the Norsemen. This old grave-stone from Orkney provides another clue. Do you notice the first name? Norse first names like this are still common in the Northern Isles. If you went to Orkney, for instance, you might meet girls with first names like Inga, Ingrid, and Thora, or boys with names like Erlend, Rognvald, Sigurd, and Thorfinn.

Most place-names, too, show a Norse origin. In Lerwick the *wick* part of the name comes from the Norse word *vik,* which means a bay or an inlet. Another word with a similar meaning is *voe.* The beach on the right, where the boats are drawn up, is Hamnavoe on one of the Shetland islands. Hamnavoe means a sheltered bay or haven. Below you can see Weisdale Voe, a large firth or inlet also in Shetland. From what you can see in the pictures, do you think these places are well named?

Look at the farm-sign from Orkney in the picture below. Like very many of the names of farms and villages in both Orkney and Shetland, it is derived from the Norse. At the bottom of the page there is a map of the north-west corner of Mainland, the largest of the islands of Orkney. On it are a number of place-names, mostly Norse. Find one that ends in *wick,* and see if you can discover how it got its name. There are also two farms with names that are modern and clearly not Norse. Can you spot them?

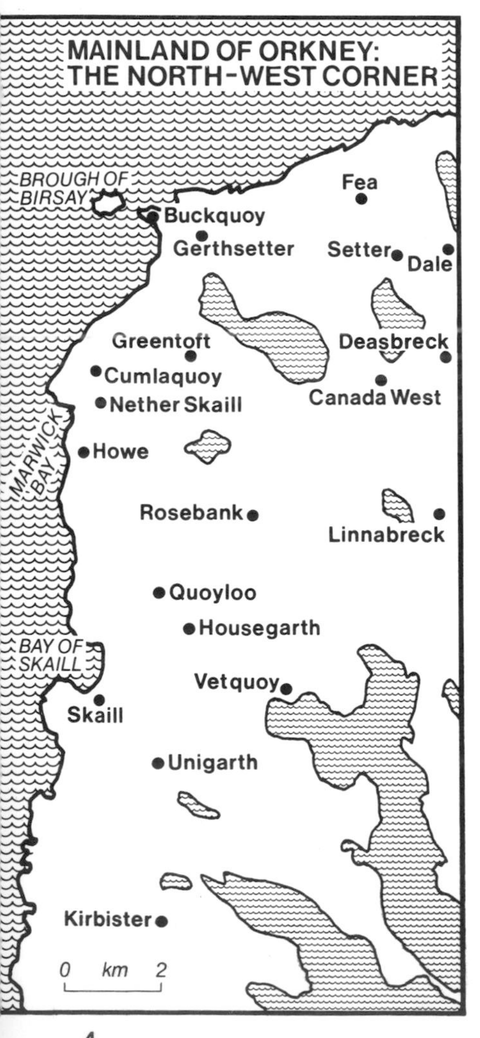

To us old place-names can seem very strange, but they are usually simple and practical descriptions of particular places. This becomes quite clear when you find out what the Orkney farm names really mean. Here is a list of meanings to help you. You should be able to discover what *Feolquoy* means.

bist or *bister*	a farm
breck	slope of a hill
dale	a valley
feol or *fea*	a fell or hill
garth or *gerth*	a dyke or enclosure
howe	a mound
quoy	an enclosure for animals
setter	a dwelling
skaill	a hall or large house
toft	a house site or small hill

Why do you think names like *garth* and *quoy* are so common?

In later years many people from other parts of Scotland went to live in the Northern Isles. Nowadays the people are a mixture, some with names that are Scottish and some that were originally Norse. It is several hundred years, too, since the Old Norse language died out as a spoken language. Now only some dialect words remain. Yet even today Orcadians and Shetlanders are proud of their Viking past. The picture at the top of the page shows how the Shetlanders remember their Viking forebears.

The Up-Helly-A' festival. The Vikings did not wear winged helmets like the men in the picture, but close-fitting round iron helmets.

Each winter, near the end of January, the people of Lerwick hold a fire festival called Up-Helly-A'. Large numbers of people dress up as Vikings, and march through the streets dragging an imitation Norse longship. At a given signal, the guisers, as they are called, throw the flaming torches they have been carrying into the ship. As the vessel burns, the guisers gather round to sing this song:

The Lerwick Galley Song

Floats the raven banner o'er us,
Round our Dragon Ship we stand,
Voices joined in gladsome chorus,
Raised aloft the flaming brand.

Worthy sons of Vikings make us,
Truth be our encircling fire
Shadowy visions backward take us,
To the Sea-king's funeral pyre.

Can you see in the picture the raven banner referred to in the song?

Up-Helly-A' continues the ancient practice of having some kind of fire festival in the depth of winter, when the nights are at their longest. Probably the fires were originally lit to drive away evil spirits. Formerly in Lerwick it was barrels of tar that were burned. Then, at the end of the nineteenth century, a model Viking galley or longship was burned instead, and this has been the practice ever since.

In burning their galley the Shetlanders are copying the Vikings, who sometimes cremated important chieftains. When a chieftain died, the goods he would need in the next life were placed in the funeral pyre to be burned with him. Not all Viking chieftains were cremated. Many were buried instead.

This photograph shows a Viking longship, the Gokstad ship from Norway, when it was excavated at the end of the last century. In this ship, around the year 900, a middle-aged man had been buried, and a huge burial-mound or howe raised over his grave. We do not know who he was, but he too may have been a sea-king.

2. Raiders and settlers

To think about

1 *To sail from Norway to Shetland, would you sail north, south, east or west?*

2 *Suggest reasons why the Norsemen were excellent boat-builders and sailors. The map on page 8 may help you with your answer.*

To find out

3 *Suppose you are the leader of a party of Norse settlers going to Scotland. Make a list of all the things you would take with you. Which ship would you choose—a knorr or a longship?*

4 *Find out about the other countries the Vikings sailed to. Draw a map showing some of the journeys that the Vikings made.*

To do

5 *Either write a story or draw a cartoon strip about a Viking raid on a lonely monastery.*

6 *Make a model of a longship, using stiff paper to make the hull.*

To find out how and why Orkney and Shetland became Norse, we have to go back in time—about 1200 years. Around the year 800, Viking raiders came from over the sea to attack the lands of western Europe. These raids and conquests happened at a time when many people migrated or moved from one land to another. Overcrowding at home was one important cause of these migrations. There were too many people in the Scandinavian homelands of the Vikings, the lands we now know as Norway, Denmark and Sweden. Many Norsemen, therefore, sailed west-over-sea (as they termed it) to seek their fortunes elsewhere.

Because of their skill as boat-builders and as seamen, the Vikings were accustomed to making long voyages. According to circumstances, they could be pirates, traders, or settlers. It was as pirates, though, that the Norsemen came to be feared. In their fast and beautifully-built longships, they brought terror and devastation to the peoples of Britain and other lands.

Isolated monasteries like Lindisfarne and Iona were obvious targets for raiders who were out for loot. In 793 Lindisfarne was attacked. Then two years later Iona suffered the first of several attacks. Since the raiders came from the sea, they had the advantage of surprise. If the place was too well defended, the Vikings could sail away again as quickly as they came. It was no wonder that people prayed to be spared from *the fury of the Northmen.* Those ships which had a dragon-head at the prow must have been especially terrifying. You can see one roughly sketched on this stone found at Jarlshof in Shetland. The stone-carving from Lindisfarne (at the top of the page) shows how the Vikings must have appeared to their victims.

But the Northmen were not just ferocious sea-robbers. They were also traders and settlers. They needed merchant ships that were broad enough and deep enough to carry either trading goods or cattle and horses for settlers going to new lands. In such cargo-boats, or *knorrs,* Vikings seamen voyaged to places as far distant as Greenland and North America.

Once a route became well known, sailing directions were passed from one mariner to another. To sail to Greenland, sailors were advised:

> 'From Herne Island (near Bergen), sail due west. Keep to the north of Shetland, but stay close enough so that, when the weather is clear, the islands are just visible. Then steer so far to the south of the Faroes that the sea seems to be midway up the mountains, and maintain your course past Iceland, staying one day's sail to the south.'

Like the Europeans who colonised America and Canada in more recent times, the Vikings sought land where they could till the soil and settle with their families. Empty, or nearly empty, lands like Iceland, the Faroe islands, and Greenland proved attractive to Norse colonists. But countries that were already inhabited were also invaded. Norwegians settled in parts of northern England and eastern Ireland, and the Danes conquered a large part of eastern England, which came to be called the Danelaw.

Below: *The remains of a knorr have been discovered at Roskilde fjord, Denmark. This is what it may have looked like. In the middle was the hold where food, water and cargo were stored. The mast, carrying a big square sail, was in the centre. The captain stood at the back and steered the ship with a huge steering oar.*

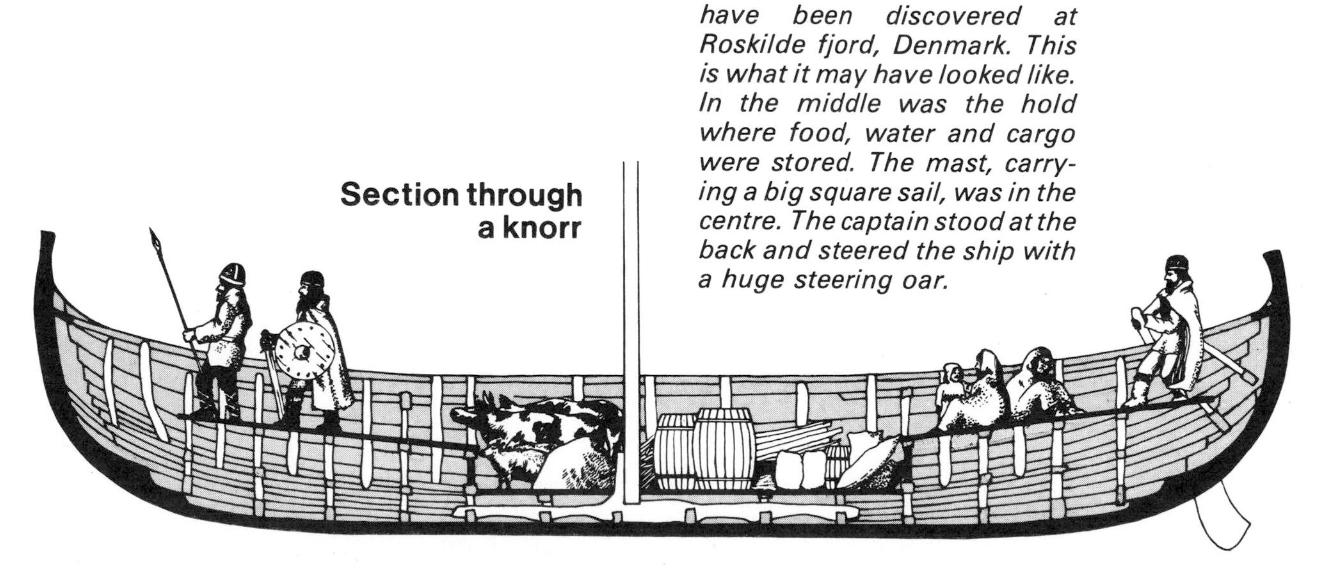

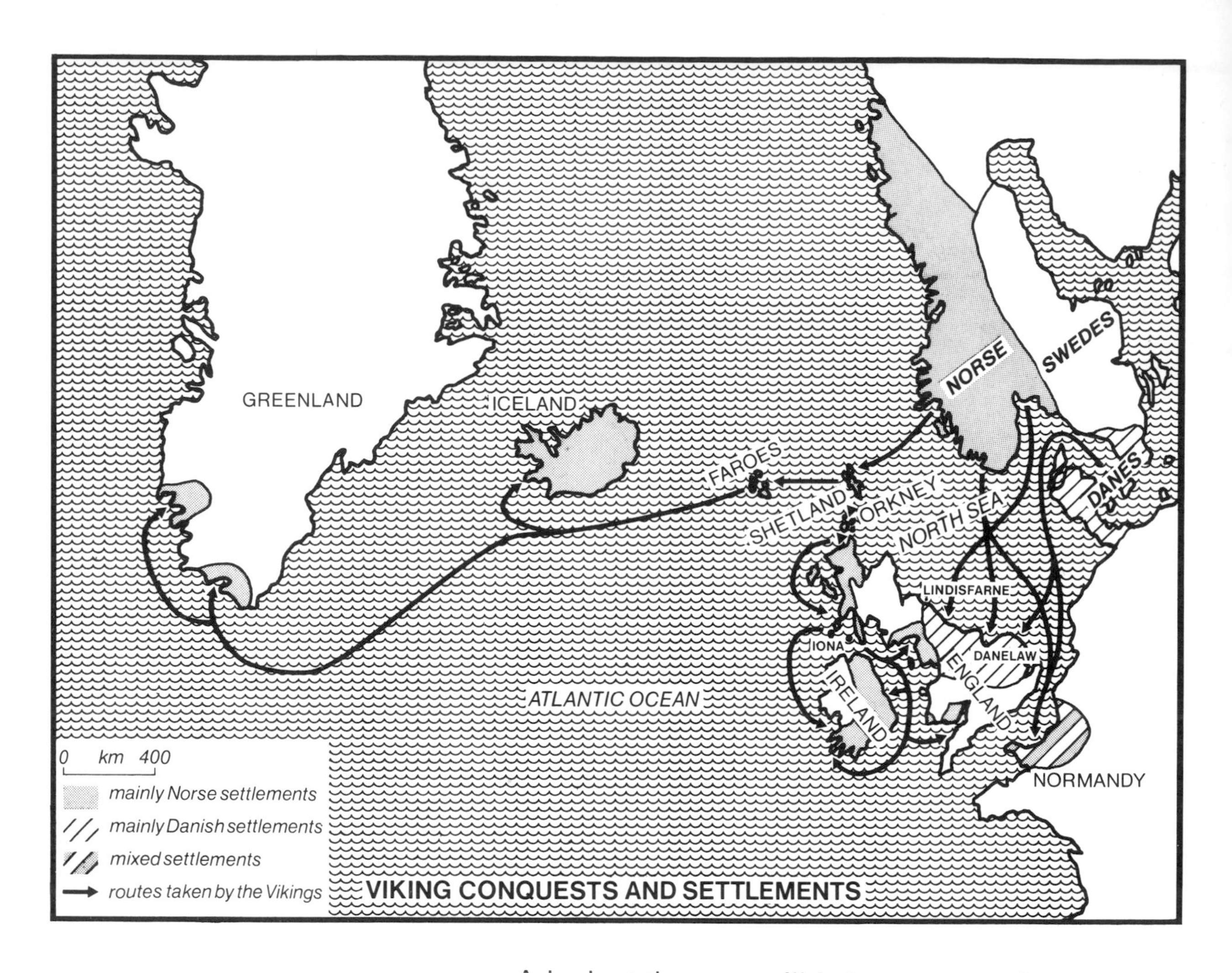

A look at the map will help you to understand why Orkney and Shetland came under the control of the Norsemen. At the closest point, the distance between Norway and Shetland is about 330 km. Since the Vikings reckoned that they could sail over 150 km in a day, you can calculate how long a time was needed to cross the North Sea to Shetland. And with a strong wind behind them, an even faster time could be achieved.

When the Vikings invaded Orkney and Shetland, the islands were inhabited by the Picts. The Picts, it would seem, did not put up much of a fight, so the Norse conquered the islands rather easily. The Norse conquest, however, has left modern historians with an unsolved problem. We simply cannot say for sure what happened to the Picts after the Norse took control of the islands. While some of the Picts continued to live in the islands, it is possible that they were kept as mere servants or slaves.

On the right you can see some bone pins of Pictish design found in a Norse dwelling at Buckquoy in Orkney. Can you suggest different possible explanations for their presence there?

Certainly the newcomers would have been glad to have the services of people with special skills. This wooden tool-box of Celtic design, which was found in an Orkney peat-bog, shows that there were some fine craftsmen working in the islands before the Norsemen arrived.

We can imagine the panic caused by the first Norse invaders. Perhaps the tool-box was dropped by a panic-stricken fugitive. If time allowed, jewellery and other valuables would have been hurriedly hidden. You can see precious objects that were buried for this reason in the picture below. The hoard was discovered under the floor of a ruined church in St Ninian's Isle in Shetland. It was a school-boy helping the archaeologists who first came upon the treasure.

But who had been the owner of this treasure? We can only guess. Perhaps it was a Pictish chieftain like this warrior carved on a stone found at Birsay in Orkney. What do you think? One thing is sure—whoever buried the treasure did not return to claim it again; we just have to imagine what his fate might have been. Perhaps he was killed, or maybe he was carried away to be sold as a slave.

Yet it is a mistake to think of the Vikings as always killing and looting. Not all monasteries and churches were rich, so most monks and priests were probably left unharmed. On this carved Pictish stone you can see the kind of priests that the Norsemen would have found in the Northern Isles. The Vikings who settled in Orkney and Shetland, it seems, did not interfere with these priests or *papae* as they called them. Papil in Shetland, where this stone comes from, is Norse for priests' homestead.

A number of other place-names derive from this Norse word for a priest. Papa Stour in Shetland and Papa Stronsay and Papa Westray in Orkney are islands where monks or hermits must have lived. The aerial photograph on the left shows the island of Papa Westray.

Once Norse settlers were established in Orkney and Shetland, Harald Finehair, the king of Norway, sailed west and, around 900, made the islands part of his kingdom. He made one of his followers, Sigurd by name, earl of Orkney, and left him to control the islands on his behalf. For hundreds of years, a succession of Norse earls ruled not only Orkney and Shetland, but also parts of the Scottish mainland.

In this fourteenth-century illustration, Harald, on the right, the first ruler who could claim to rule most of Norway, is shown with his father Halfdan the Black. Notice Harald's long hair.

The Northern Isles, especially Orkney, were of great value to the Viking kings of Norway as a jumping-off point for raids on both Scotland and England. When the Norse king Harald Hardrada invaded England in 1066, he spent some time in Orkney on his way south. Two earls of Orkney, Paul and Erlend, who were the joint rulers at that time, fought on Harald's side when he was defeated by Harold Godwinson at Stamford Bridge. Unlike the Norse king, they survived the battle and were able to return to Orkney.

3. West-over-sea to Scotland

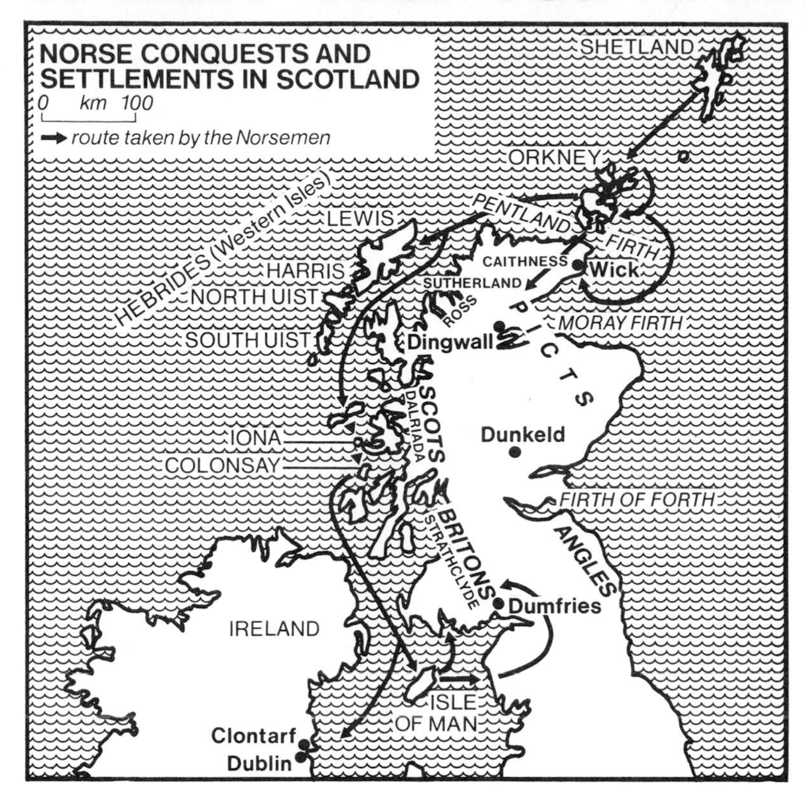

For hundreds of years the Viking raids continued. If their enemies had been united, the Norsemen would have found things more difficult. But many countries then were divided into different kingdoms, which fought one against the other. In 800 there was no Scottish nation as we know it today. In the land that we now call Scotland there were no fewer than four different peoples. In the west lived the Scots of Dalriada who were a Celtic race and had originally come from Ireland; in the south-west were Britons of Strathclyde, another Celtic people; from the Firth of Forth to the far north was the territory of the Picts; and in the south-east there were Angles.

The divisions among the peoples of Scotland gave the Vikings their opportunity. From Orkney they crossed the Pentland Firth to the Scottish mainland, and settled in Caithness. Wick is one of many places in that area which still bears a Norse name. While Caithness became part of the earldom of Orkney, the lands further south, Sutherland and Ross, were not so easily conquered. Sutherland and Ross remained a frontier zone, and the Norse made little headway there.

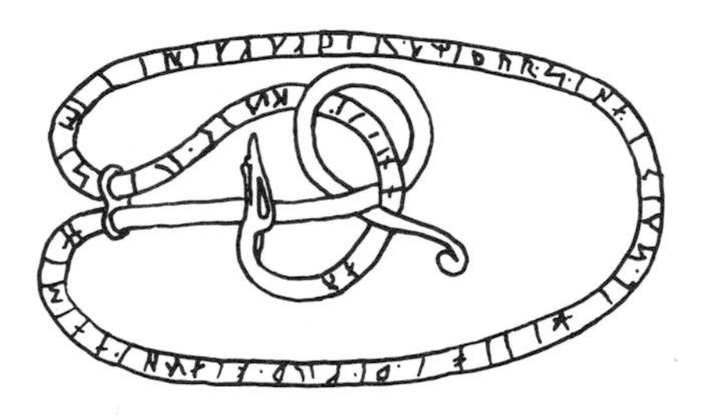

To think about

1 *Why do you think the Vikings thought of the British Isles as part of the western lands?*

2 *The Oseberg ship was old and worn when it was buried. Why do you think this was?*

To do

3 *Who were the Gall-Gaels? Who would have given them this name?*

4 *Find out what you can about Iceland. Do you think Ketil Flatnose's choice of destination was a wise one?*

To find out

5 *One of the finds shown in the picture of weapons on page 13 is a piece of chain mail. Find pictures or make drawings showing this kind of armour.*

6 *You could make some Viking chessmen using balsa wood, or a Celtic brooch using tin foil.*

7 *You could make models of the scales and weights shown on page 12. Each of the scale-pans was fixed to the balance beam by three fine chains. The original chains have been lost.*

The Oseberg ship was carefully uncovered from its burial mound by archaeologists. Here you can see the prow surrounded by the earth of the mound. A tarpaulin protects the rest of the ship.

Decorated weights (above) *and bronze scales* (below) *from the Colonsay grave*

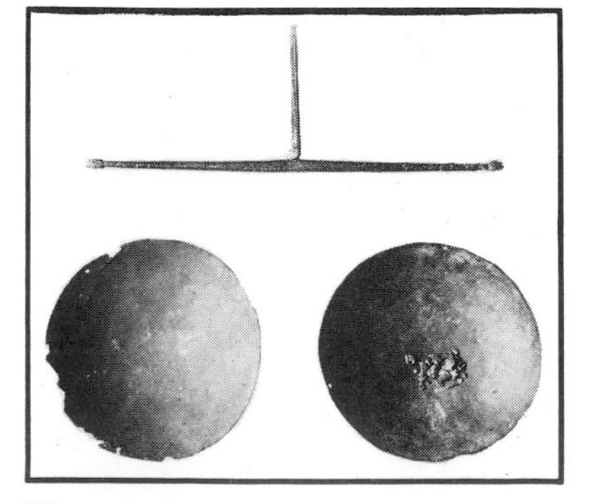

Although the Vikings were not so dominant in Sutherland and Ross, many of the place-names in these areas are Norse in origin. Sutherland itself means the southland. The town of Dingwall in Ross derives from the Norse word *thing,* which means a kind of local parliament.

The islands on the west coast of Scotland were also attacked. One after another the Hebrides or Western Isles of Scotland came under Norse control, as did the Isle of Man and part of Ireland. You can find these places on the map. Some of the Norsemen who settled in these islands, which they called the Sudreys or south islands, had been great men in their own country. The story is that they left because they felt King Harald Finehair was becoming too powerful.

The *Laxdale Saga,* which is a story about Viking settlers in Iceland, tells us about some of those Norwegians who had quarrelled with their king. Some wanted to go to Iceland, because the fishing grounds were good there. On the other hand, their leader, who was a powerful chieftain called Ketil Flatnose, had no desire to go so far north. 'That fishing place', he said 'will never see me in my old age.' He preferred to sail 'west across the sea to Scotland', where he thought he could make a good living. Ketil knew Scotland well, for he had raided far and wide in that country. Ketil was 'famous and of noble birth', and the saga says that he was welcomed by the leading men in Scotland when he arrived in his adopted land.

When Ketil said that he could make a good living in Scotland, it is probable that he meant to trade as well as raid. We can learn something of the activities of powerful chieftains like him from the contents of a grave found in Colonsay. (Colonsay, incidentally, means Kolbein's island, but we do not know anything about this particular Kolbein.) In this grave there was a skeleton of a Viking. He had been buried in a boat. Unfortunately, very little of it survived, unlike the richly carved ship which was found in a burial mound at Oseberg in Norway. In the Colonsay grave there was a horse, which had been sacrificed and then buried along with weapons and other possessions of the dead man. Among his possessions was this set of scales made of bronze. What do you think he might have used the scales for?

Over the years other Viking graves have been discovered in the Western Isles of Scotland. In them have been found peaceful items like ploughs, sickles, hammers, tongs, clippers and iron cauldrons. But the finds from the graves also include a variety of weapons—swords, spears and axes like the ones in the photograph below. It would seem that these were the graves of settlers who had to be prepared to fight to keep their lands and possessions.

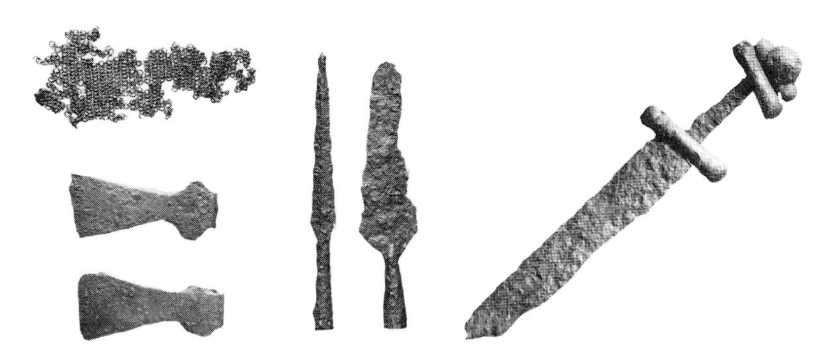

Left: *Viking weapons from Norway: axe-heads, spear-heads, a sword and fragments of chain mail*

The remains of some Norse houses have also been found in the Hebrides. When a guided weapons range was being constructed in South Uist, this boat-shaped Norse house was uncovered. No weapons were found at the site. The inhabitants were pastoral farmers, who kept cattle, sheep, pigs, and horses. Among the finds was a chopper made of whalebone. It may have been used for preparing leather. The Norsemen who lived here would have been simple peasants relying on some great chieftain for protection. But at least they would have been free men, not serfs like the peasants in many other parts of Europe.

Below: *Foundations of a Norse house, South Uist*

Whalebone chopper found near the house at South Uist

Fewer Norsemen settled in the Hebrides than in Orkney and Shetland. The Scots or Gaels remained in the majority. While some of them adopted the ways of the newcomers, most continued to speak their own language. Hebrideans, who were partly Norse, came to be called Gall-Gaels or foreign Gaels.

There was one part of the Western Isles where many Norsemen settled, and that was Lewis, the northern part of the Outer Hebrides group. As elsewhere in the Hebrides, many mountains and lochs bear names that are Norse in origin. Even more significant is the fact that most of the names of villages and crofts derive from Old Norse. Such a high proportion of Norse names shows that many Norsemen must have settled there.

Relics of the later Norse period in Lewis are these chessmen, made of walrus ivory. 178 chessmen were found in the same place. Can you identify the king, queen, bishop, knight and pawn. Look at the royal piece in the picture below. Notice the decorative carving on the back and sides of the king's throne or *high-seat.* Ornamental high-seats like these were a feature of the halls of great chieftains in the Norse lands.

Just as the Gaels were influenced by the Norse, so the Vikings in their turn adopted some of the customs of the Scots and the Irish. A story in the *Heimskringla* or *Sagas of the Norse Kings* tells how King Magnus Bareleg got his nickname.

> 'People say that when King Magnus came home from his viking cruise to the western countries (i.e. Scotland and Ireland) he and many of his men returned with many of the fashions and types of dress that were usual in the western lands. They went about on the streets with bare legs, and had short tunics and over-cloaks, and therefore his men called him Magnus Barefoot or Bareleg.'

Christianity, too, made an impact on the Vikings. Although they invaded churches in search of loot, some Norsemen were so impressed by the Christian faith that they became Christians themselves. Among the converts was Aud, the daughter of Ketil Flatnose. Her brother Bjorn, however, did not approve of her conversion. His view was that only feeble-minded people became Christians.

Not all the Norsemen who went to Scotland stayed there permanently. Bjorn, for instance, did not share his father's preference for Scotland. He soon left the Hebrides and settled in Iceland. Many years later Aud decided to follow his example. One of her sons had been treacherously slain, so she thought Iceland might be a safer place for her family. This remarkable woman, therefore, ordered the ship for her journey to be made secretly in a forest in Caithness.

Aud's treasure probably included brooches like the one shown here. This brooch, which was found at Hunterston in Ayrshire, is a fine example of Celtic jewellery of this period. Though it was made by a Scottish or Irish craftsman, it was later owned by a

Norseman. We know this because, scratched on the back, there are some Viking runes. Runes were a form of alphabet used by the Vikings.

The back of the Hunterston brooch. Can you see the runes?

Many other Hebrideans took the same route as Bjorn and Aud. Quite a number of the present-day inhabitants of Iceland, and of the Faroe Islands too, are descended from immigrants from the Western Isles and other parts of Scotland. Some, like Bjorn and Aud, went of their own accord. Many others were Scots who had been captured in battle and were taken to Iceland as slaves. Some, in course of time, were freed by their captors. It is related in the *Laxdale Saga* how Aud gave grants of land to some of her servants: 'Another of her freed slaves was called Hundi, a Scotsman by birth; to him she granted Hundadale.'

The Viking invasions affected Scotland in a number of ways. The kingdom of the Picts was greatly weakened by the attacks of both Norsemen and Danes. Having one common enemy, however, helped to bring the Scots and Picts together. About 843 a new and united kingdom of Alba came into being, when Kenneth MacAlpin became king of both Picts and Scots.

Since Iona was too easily attacked from the sea, its treasures were removed to the monastery of Kells in Ireland, and Dunkeld became the headquarters of the Scottish church. Nevertheless, monks continued to live on Iona, and the island was still regarded as an exceptionally holy place. For a long time to come kings and other important people were taken there for burial. As late as the sixteenth century Highland chieftains were still being buried at Iona. You can see some of their gravestones in this picture.

Left: *Gravestones of medieval Highland chieftains at Iona*

 **To think about**

1 *Would you say that the pagan Vikings believed in a life after death? Give reasons for your answer.*

 **To find out**

2 *Look closely at the photograph at the bottom of the page. Can you see the grave-goods? What could they be used for?*

3 *Look at a map of south-west Scotland and north-west England. Can you find some places whose names were originally Norse?*

 **To do**

4 *You could read* The Shield Ring, *by Rosemary Sutcliff, a story about the Norse in the Lake District.*

5 *Make a list, with drawings, of the different kinds of objects that an archaeologist might find in a Viking warrior's grave.*

6 *Write an imaginative story telling how the Skaill treasure hoard came to be hidden.*

4. How we know: archaeological evidence and place-names

In this chapter we see how historians find answers to problems by studying archaeological evidence and place-names. The next chapter deals with other kinds of evidence such as written records and traditional stories like sagas.

Over the years archaeologists have uncovered a great deal of evidence. This has given us information about Viking ships, houses, weapons, and ornaments. Oddly enough, we can learn a lot about the life of the Vikings from the way they treated their dead. When someone was buried, it was common practice for personal possessions to be placed in the grave also. If the dead person was of high rank, then these *grave-goods* were often of great value. Even horses and dogs were sometimes buried or burned with their owner.

Here is a picture of a Norse grave unearthed at Gurness in Orkney. In it the archaeologists discovered two bronze brooches (which were usually worn in pairs), a necklace made of sea-shells, a knife with a wooden handle, and a small iron sickle. You can see the brooches below. Now pretend you are an archaeologist. Would you say that this was the grave of a man or a woman?

An even richer grave was discovered on the island of Rousay in Orkney. In the grave was found this fine brooch, made of silver and gold with amber studs. It was probably made by an Irish craftsman.

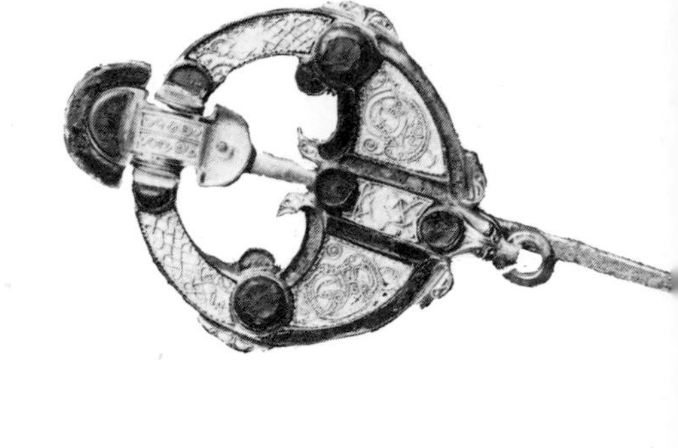

Occasionally, a chance discovery can provide important archaeological evidence. In 1858 a boy was hunting rabbits near the Bay of Skaill in Orkney. Chasing one rabbit to its burrow, the boy noticed some odd-shaped objects that had been scraped up by the rabbits. A close examination of the objects revealed that they were made of silver. The boy had stumbled on a hoard of treasure that had been concealed in the sand for about 900 years. Ninety silver objects, including coins, were unearthed. On the right you can see some of the finds from the Skaill treasure hoard: arm-rings, neck-rings, and brooches. Can you identify them? The large brooches were used to fasten cloaks. You can see the pin which kept the cloak in place.

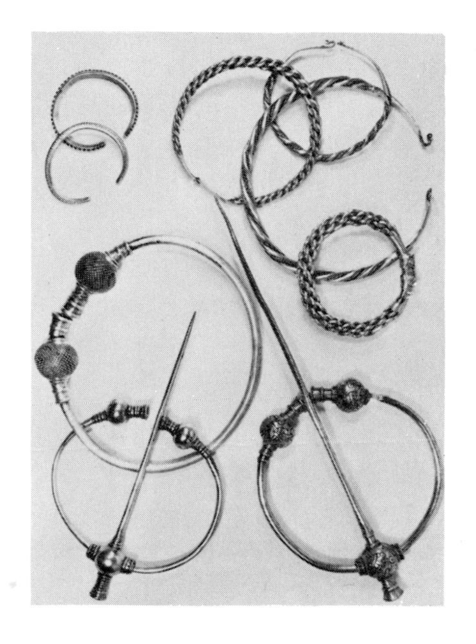

In the Skaill hoard were a number of English and Arabic coins. The dates of these coins suggest that the treasure was probably hidden between the years 950 and 1000. While some of the coins might have been plunder, others could possibly have been exchanged for trade goods. The Vikings, it is important to remember, were not just pirates; they were also successful traders and merchants.

Left: *English and Arabic coins from the Skaill treasure hoard*

You will notice that some of the coins have been broken. For the Vikings it was the weight of silver that mattered. If a Viking was making a small purchase, then he would pay with a piece of silver cut from a coin. Sometimes coins and other silver objects were melted down to be made into ring-money—simple bracelets or arm-rings, parts of which could be broken off when required for a purchase. On the left you can see two pieces of ring-money, found in the Skaill treasure hoard. Accurate scales and weights were therefore necessary, especially for merchants. On page 12 you saw the scales and weights found in the Viking grave at Colonsay.

While hoards of treasure might belong to any period, grave-goods generally belong only to the early period of Norse settlement. Leaving the dead with some of their belongings was a pagan custom. When the Vikings became Christians, this practice died out. In fact, the presence or absence of grave-goods helps us to know when different peoples became Christian.

The new methods of burial are described in the *Saga of Eric the Red.* When Eric's son Thorstein died, his corpse came back to life long enough to issue a last request. This request, which was given to his wife, was that he wished to be buried in consecrated or holy ground.

> 'It's a bad custom to bury people in unholy ground with scarcely any funeral rites as has been done in Greenland since Christianity came here. I want to be taken to church, along with the other people who have died here.'

In this picture you can see small statues of some of the gods the Vikings worshipped before they became Christians. There are lucky charms shaped like the hammer of Thor, who was the god of Thunder. Also in this collection, which is from Sweden, there are some crucifixes or crosses. Can you tell which of the objects are Christian?

As we have already seen, place-names are clues which help us to find out exactly where the Vikings settled. We find that in the south-west of Scotland, round about Dumfries, there are many place-names that have a Norse origin. We can also tell that the Vikings who settled there had not come directly from Norway. They had migrated from earlier Norse colonies which had been established in the north of England. In other words, the Norse in the Dumfries area were an overflow from settlements further south in Cumbria and Lancashire. We know this because there are many place-names that are common to both the south-west of Scotland and the north-west of England. These include words like *beck,* meaning a stream, and *by* or *bie* meaning a village or group of houses.

5. How we know: chronicles and sagas

Much of what we know about the Vikings comes from what people wrote about them either at the time or in later centuries. In some chronicles (records of events, written by monks) there are occasional references to the Vikings. These mainly relate to raids and attacks, which, not surprisingly, the Christian scholars regarded as horrifying. This is what one angry monk wrote after learning of the attack on the monastery of Lindisfarne, which had been made famous by St Cuthbert:

> 'Never before has such terror appeared in Britain as has now been inflicted upon us by the heathens. Nor was it believed that such an invasion from the sea could be made. The church of St Cuthbert is spattered with blood and all its ornaments spoiled. The pagans have taken for their prey the holiest place in the whole of Britain.'

The monasteries of Lindisfarne and Iona were later rebuilt. This photograph shows the ruins of the medieval monastery of Lindisfarne, rebuilt three hundred years after the Viking attack.

For more detailed information about the Vikings we have to turn to the great sagas of Iceland. These started as stories that were told in the long, dark winter evenings. In the chiefs' halls, in different parts of Iceland, groups would gather round the fire to hear tales of famous people and great events. But not all the stories concerned the great and the famous. The Icelanders were also eager to learn about their own and neighbours' ancestors. They wanted to know how their forefathers had come to Iceland and to learn about their deeds and achievements. Over the years the saga tales were passed on by word of mouth from one generation to the next. Centuries later these traditional stories were written down by Icelandic scholars, and so a great deal of valuable information about the Vikings and their times was preserved.

To think about

1 *In the castle illustrated on page 20 you can see the entrance to an underground storage tank. What purpose do you think it served?*

To find out

2 *Find other stories from the Icelandic sagas. You could read* The Burning of Njal *by Henry Treece. It is a short version of one of the most famous sagas.*

To do

3 *Write a play about Vikings breaking into a howe. You could record it on a tape-recorder with sound effects.*

We cannot accept as true everything written in the sagas. Stories told and retold over a long period of time never end up the same as they started, and some of the traditional tales in the sagas were no doubt exaggerated to make a better story. Still, much of the saga record can be confirmed from other sources. Archaeologists and historians have been able to prove that some of the places, buildings. and people mentioned in the sagas actually did exist.

One Viking chieftain mentioned in the sagas is Kolbein Hruga, who lived on the isle of Wyre in Orkney. On that small island, according to the *Orkneyinga Saga,* he 'had a fine stone castle built there, which was a safe stronghold'. This was at a time when stone castles were rare, and so Kolbein's castle must have been one of the earliest to be built in Scotland. Since Kolbein Hruga was described as a very overbearing man, perhaps he had need of it. Oddly enough, eight centuries later his name was still remembered on Wyre, although it now was in the local dialect form of 'Cubbie Roo'. Yet, his stone castle had long since disappeared. All that remained was an earthen mound, which was known to locals as Cubbie Roo's castle. When archaeologists investigated this site, sure enough under the mound were found the remains of a stone tower.

Cubbie Roo's castle, Wyre

As you can see, it was very small, but its walls were strong enough to withstand a siege in 1231, some eighty years after it had been built by Kolbein Hruga. This was when, according to *King Hakon's Saga,* the killers of an Orkney earl escaped to Wyre 'and took refuge in the castle which Kolbein Hruga had built there'. The friends of the dead earl followed them there, but found it 'a difficult place to attack'.

As *Hruga* means 'a heap', Kolbein Hruga must have been a big, strong man. In his case we can see how fact became transformed into legend. Centuries after his death, none of the local people could remember Kolbein Hruga. Instead, tales were told of a giant, who in the mythical past had been responsible for some remarkable feats which had needed great strength. It seems, therefore, that over a long period of time the real-life Kolbein Hruga became transformed into the giant known as Cubbie Roo.

From the sagas we learn that the Norsemen were fond of pranks and dare-devil adventures. One favourite dare involved breaking into ancient burial mounds, or *'howe-breaking'* as they termed it. Since they believed that such howes were inhabited by the spirits of the dead, this did take some courage. The sagas are full of tales of hauntings and unearthly acts. An additional lure was the hope of finding the treasure which these prehistoric burial places were supposed to contain.

One obvious target in Orkney was Maes Howe, the largest of the many Stone Age burial mounds or cairns to be found in these fertile islands. On the right you can see the outside and the inside of Maes Howe. Some Viking warriors, the *Orkneyinga Saga* tells us, took refuge there during a snow-storm. What exactly happened we do not know; but their journey was delayed, as two of the band were 'seized with madness'.

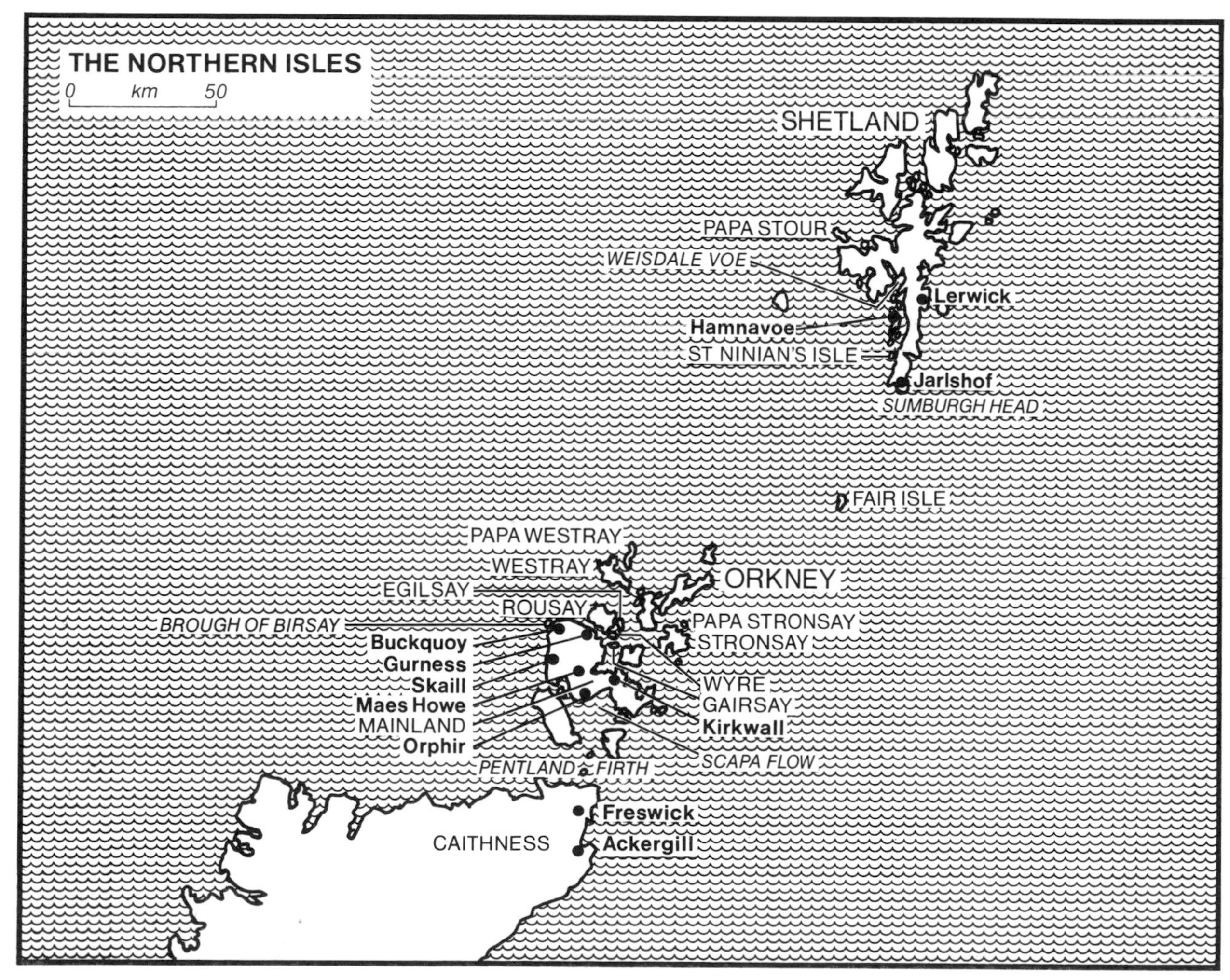

These warriors were not the first Vikings to enter the cairn. When archaeologists first explored the interior over one hundred years ago, the chambers inside were found to be empty. Any valuables or other objects that the tombs may have contained had long since been removed. Relics of a different kind were found, however. A large number of runes had been carved on the stone walls of the largest chamber. (As we saw in chapter 3, runes were the form of alphabet the Vikings used). Many of these were just scribbles, saying things like 'Helgi was here'. Two of them mention that pilgrims who were on their way to Jerusalem broke into the tomb.

Runes carved on the wall at Maes Howe

We know of these pilgrims from the *Orkneyinga Saga,* which is an account of the deeds of the Earls of Orkney. One of those earls, Rognvald by name, led an expedition which left Norway for the Holy Land in 1151. On their way to the east, they stopped off in Orkney to spend the winter there and thus avoid the winter gales. These Jerusalem-farers, as they were called, seemed to have been rather uproarious characters. As the saga writer puts it:

> 'There was a great turmoil in the Islands; the Orkneymen and the Norwegians quarrelled frequently about bargains, and women, and other things. The Earl had a very difficult task to keep peace among them.'

Judging by the *Orkneyinga Saga,* howe-breaking was one of the tamer exploits of that rather unruly band of pilgrims.

Some of the runes in Maes Howe refer to treasure having been removed by persons who had earlier broken into the howe. One of the inscriptions states that there was still treasure to be found, another says that 'away to the north-west is a great treasure hidden'.

To modern archaeologists Maes Howe itself with its Norse inscriptions is the real 'treasure'. Among the Norsemen who broke into this cairn was one who was a remarkably fine artist. We do not know who he was, but he left his memorial in the form of this carving. Some say it is meant to be a dragon; others describe it as a lion. What do you think?

6. Jarlshof - a Viking settlement

Earl Rognvald Kolson was soaked through to the skin. Shivering, he crouched close to the fire and tried to dry himself. Just then Asa, a servant girl who had been sent to the well to fetch water, entered the farm-house. She had fallen into a pool in the dark, so she, too, was soaking wet. When she tried to explain what had happened her teeth chattered so much that no-one could understand her. But the earl understood her plight. The verse he composed on the spur of the moment expressed his sympathy.

Asa! you seem quite exhausted.
Atatata! You've been drenched with water.
Hutututu! Where shall I sit?
By the fire—I'm frozen through and through.

The earl was the same Rognvald who led the expedition to the Holy Land. This incident, however, took place some years earlier. Rognvald had been on his way back from Norway to Orkney, when he was shipwrecked off Shetland. Fortunately, he and his men got ashore safely and made their way to some farmhouses, where they were able to get shelter.

We know of this story because it was written down in the *Orkneyinga Saga,* but we cannot say for sure where it happened. However, we can examine the remains of a similar type of Norse settlement at Jarlshof near Sumburgh Head in Shetland. From this remarkable site, we can learn a great deal about everyday life and work in the Viking Age. Thus, archaeological evidence is used to supplement the saga record, the two together giving us a more complete picture than we would otherwise have.

Jarlshof, excavated in the 1930s, is a unique site. Archaeologists have found at this spot a whole succession of settlements, stretching as far back as the Bronze Age. In this photograph you can see, in the foreground, the foundations of some Norse buildings, and, in the background, the ruins of a sixteenth-century laird's house.

To think about

1 *Can you identify the tools and other equipment being used by the blacksmith and his assistant (page 26)?*

To find out

2 *Find out from the map where Jarlshof is. How can you tell that this was a good place for a settlement?*

3 *What can you learn about life and work at Jarlshof from the drawing on pages 24 and 25?*

To do

4 *Draw, or write a story about, the Viking buried at Buckquoy.*

5 *Make a model of a Norse farm.*

The Norsemen, who arrived about 800, were to occupy this site for some four hundred years, enlarging and altering the lay-out several times during their long occupation. Here is an artist's impression of the settlement in its early years. The farmhouse or long-house is on the left. Close to it stood a small building, which may have served as a bath-house of the sauna type. The building on the extreme right of the picture served either as a barn or a cow-shed. Next to it was the smithy or blacksmith's workshop.

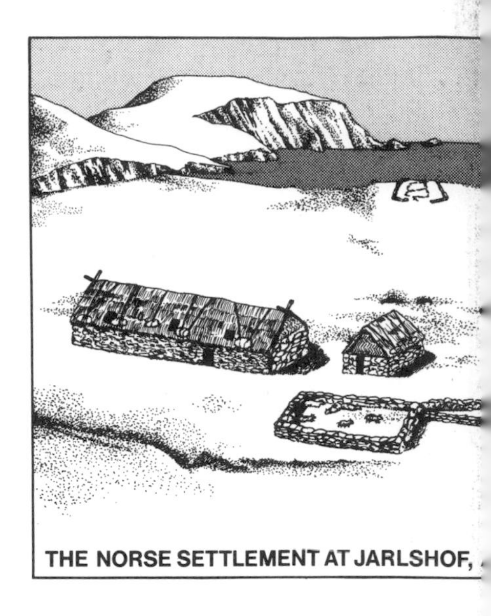
THE NORSE SETTLEMENT AT JARLSHOF,

The first settlers built their farmhouse according to a traditional Norse design. But they had to use different material. As timber was scarce, turf and stone had to be used instead. The house, which was 21 metres long, had two rooms—a large living-room and a small kitchen.

In the middle of the main room was a long stone-lined fireplace, similar to the Orkney one in the picture at the bottom of this page. We can imagine Earl Rognvald and his companions warming themselves around such a hearth. Being a farmer's house, the furniture would have been poor and simple—a few stools, benches, and low tables. When it was time for bed, the Norsemen stayed in the same room. All they had to do was stack up the furniture and unroll the bed-clothes.

In the kitchen there was another open fireplace and a stone oven. But oddly enough there was no fireplace under the oven. Just think about this. How can you cook anything in a cold oven? Yet it had been used. When the excavation was carried out, there

Below: *Norse house on the Brough of Birsay. Can you see the remains of the fireplace in the centre of the room?*

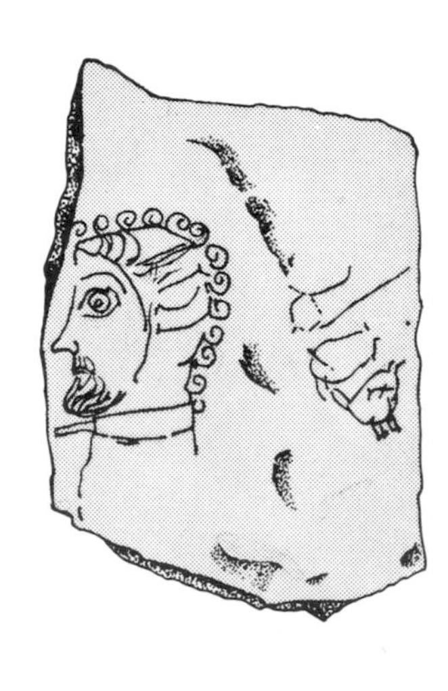

THE YEAR 800

were still a lot of fish-bones inside the oven. These settlers must have been rather fond of baked fish.

Actually the heat for the oven was provided in a rather clumsy fashion. This is how it was done. The cook first put some small stones into the fire. When they were hot they were rolled into the oven. (This must have been a risky business.) Then damp grass was laid on the hot stones to keep the food from burning. Next, in went the food, which was covered by another layer of grass. Lastly, the cook pushed more hot stones on top of everything. The contents of the oven must have looked rather like a large sandwich.

The presence of stone sinkers for fishing lines is another indication that these Norsemen were accustomed to fishing. Yet, in spite of their closeness to the shore, it seems that farming for the first settlers was a more important activity than fishing. Bones found on the site indicate that they kept sheep, cattle, pigs and ponies.

As the years went past, the settlement was extended. Although some buildings were demolished, new ones were added. The drawing on the left shows how Jarlshof must have appeared after several centuries of Norse settlement. By that time, fishing had become a major occupation. But, as you can see, farming was still important. Can you find the byre or cow-shed in this illustration? Leading up to its entrance is a narrow cattle-road, with a low wall on either side. If you look again at the picture on page 23, you can see a bit of the cattle-road and the foundations of the byre. Notice, too, the central pavement.

We know what some of the people at Jarlshof looked like from drawings left on slates and pieces of stone. It was quite a skilled artist who sketched the man's head shown on page 24. The drawing above is incomplete, as the slate must have broken. Notice the knot in the animal's tail. What do you think the artist was trying to depict in the drawing on the left?

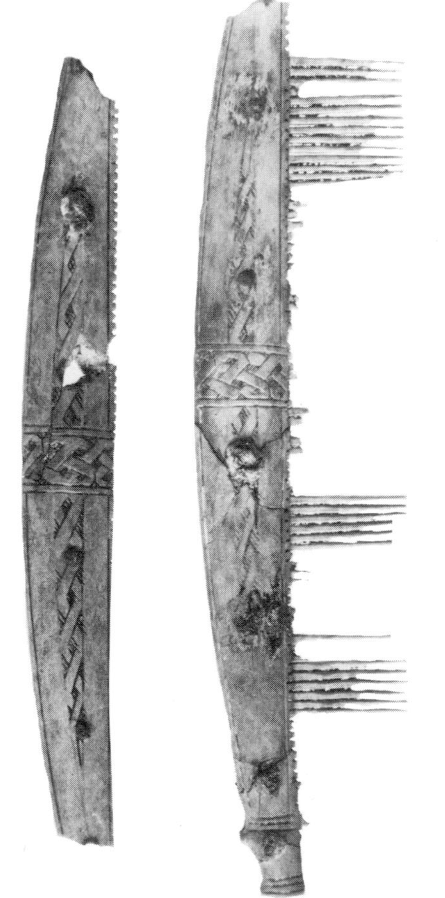

This wooden carving from Norway shows two men at work in a smithy. The Norsemen at Jarlshof had to be largely self-reliant, using their own produce to feed themselves. They made their own tools and most of their utensils. We know they used iron because iron knives, sickles and nails have been found. These would have been forged in their own smithy, which the archaeologists were able to identify by the presence of a hearth, a stone anvil and lumps of iron slag.

Other everyday objects like combs and hair-pins also had to be home-made. They were fashioned out of bones or antlers. Some of these objects, like the broken combs on the left, were finely carved.

No pottery was found at Jarlshof. Instead of making pottery, the Norsemen carved jugs and containers from a soft stone called soapstone or steatite. Until a quarry was discovered in Shetland itself, steatite pots had to be imported from Norway.

Although we often think of the Vikings as ferocious marauders, life at Jarlshof seems to have been fairly peaceful. Very few weapons were found and these belong to the earliest period of settlement. All the traces are of peaceful pursuits—of the tools and equipment needed to win a livelihood from the land and the sea. Almost certainly, though, passing long-ships would have stopped to take on food and water. The remains of camp fires down at the shore probably indicate where their crews encamped. Perhaps the sea-rovers now and again recruited some adventurous lad, who was eager to leave the settlement to try to make his fortune in strange and foreign lands.

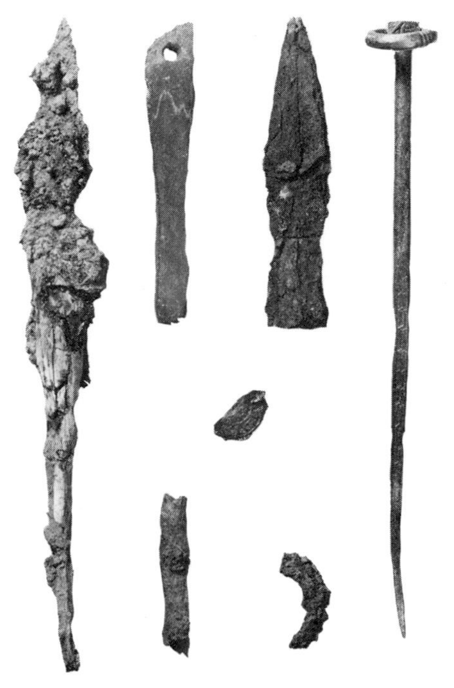

Traces of other Viking settlements have been found in Scotland, at Ackergill and Freswick in Caithness and at Buckquoy and Brough of Birsay in Orkney. At Buckquoy a Norse longhouse overlay a Pictish farm-house. The objects illustrated here are from a Viking grave found on that site. From left to right they are a rusted iron knife, a whetstone for sharpening weapons, an iron spearhead, a bronze pin; in the centre is part of an Anglo-Saxon coin, a silver penny minted during the reign of King Edmund; and the other objects are a strip of bone with two iron rivets, which was probably part of the sheath which would have gone with the knife, and, lastly, part of the iron buckle for the dead man's belt. Below you can see the bone handle which probably fitted the knife.

All these items can give you an idea of the kind of objects a Norse warrior would have carried. Try to imagine him in his homespun clothes, with his cloak fastened with the long pin, a spear in one hand, and round his waist a belt with his knife and whetstone fastened to it. He was almost certainly a pagan, since it was not Christian practice to put personal belong-ings into a grave. Since Edmund reigned as king of England from 939 to 946, the grave can be dated to some time after 940.

7. Sigurd the Fat and Thorfinn the Mighty

To think about

1 *Look carefully at the aerial photograph of the Brough of Birsay. Do you think that it was a suitable place for Earl Thorfinn's palace?*

To find out

2 *Find stories or poems about the old Viking gods.*

3 *Try to find out the details of the battle of Stamford Bridge.*

To do

4 *Make up a play or a wall newspaper dealing with one of the events in this chapter.*

5 *Make a Viking standard for yourself, choosing a raven, a dragon, or something similar.*

About the year 1000, the earl of Orkney was Sigurd the Fat, who, in spite of his name, was a mighty warrior. His rule, it is said, extended even to the Isle of Man. In the sagas a number of strange tales are told concerning the Earl Sigurd. One tells of a chance encounter between the earl and Olaf Tryggvason, who was king of Norway from 995 to 1000. Having been converted to Christianity himself, Olaf tried to compel other Norsemen to follow his example. Those who refused had to suffer the consequences.

The story starts with Olaf returning from a war-cruise. At the head of a mighty fleet, he sailed into Orkney waters, where he took Sigurd by surprise, and captured him and some of his men. For Olaf it was just the opportunity he was seeking. He gave Sigurd an ultimatum: either he and his followers must become Christians or they would be killed and the islands devastated. At Olaf's mercy, the earl gave way and agreed to these terms.

Whether this particular story is true or not, we cannot say. But such episodes were not unusual. In the cathedral in Kirkwall you can see this statue of a later King Olaf. He was Olaf Haraldsson, who is now the patron saint of Norway. As this sculpture suggests, St Olaf also won converts by the sword. In the sagas there are many blood-curdling stories about the methods he employed to win converts to Christianity.

Saint Olaf

If Sigurd the Fat did become a Christian, he certainly did not take his vows too seriously. If you look again at the flag on the Up-Helly-A' longship, you will see that it shows a raven in flight. This banner is meant to be a copy of Earl Sigurd's personal standard, which was supposed to have magical powers. It had been woven 'with mighty spells', which were to ensure that Sigurd's forces would always be victorious. But there was one major drawback—whoever carried the raven standard was doomed to die.

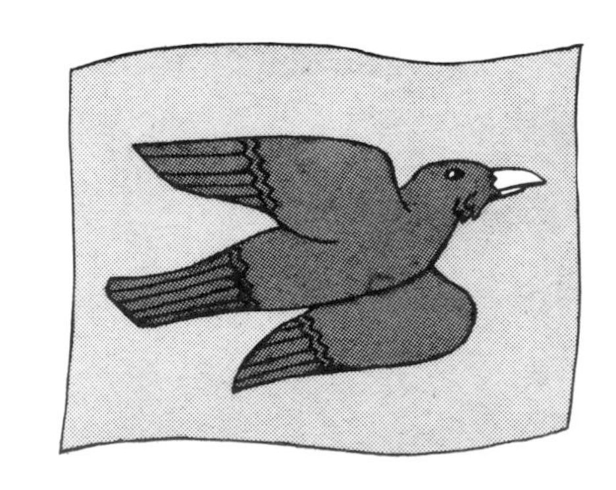

In 1014 Earl Sigurd of Orkney was campaigning in Ireland, in alliance with the Viking king of Dublin, Sigtrygg Silky-beard. On Good Friday at Clontarf near Dublin an Irish army, led by their High King, Brian Boru, confronted the Norsemen. Sigurd was one of the foremost in the fight. An Irish chronicle describes him as dealing out wounds and slaughter all around: 'neither sword nor axe could harm him'.

King Sigtrygg may have looked like this bearded chessman

Fluttering above the heads of the men of Orkney at Clontarf was the dreaded raven banner. First one standard-bearer was killed; then another. The next man was scared to carry the fatal banner, so he refused. When Hrafn the Red was ordered to take it up, he shouted back to Sigurd: 'Carry your own devil.' So the earl had to take the banner himself, and soon he too shared the fate of the others who had borne the accursed flag.

With Sigurd dead, the heart went out of the Norsemen. Many of the men of Orkney were already slain, and the survivors took refuge in flight. One of the lucky ones was Hrafn the Red, although he came close to death when he was pursued into a river. Another Viking, an Icelander, had to interrupt his flight to tie a shoe-lace. When his pursuers asked why he, too, was not running, he replied: 'Because I can't get home tonight, for my home is in Iceland.' Fortunately for him his life was spared.

The Battle of Clontarf, one of the bloodiest ever fought on Irish soil, was long remembered. The sagas tell of miracles and fearsome omens that foretold the death of many warriors. In places as far apart as Caithness, the Hebrides, the Faroes, and Iceland, various weird events were recorded on that memorable Good Friday. In Orkney, we are told, on the very day of the battle, a man called Harek, who thought he saw Earl Sigurd and some of his men, rode out to meet them.

> 'They were seen to meet and then to ride behind a hill, but they disappeared from sight. Harek was never seen again.'

Viking horseman, a chessman from Lewis

Of all the earls of Orkney, the most powerful was Thorfinn, the youngest son of Sigurd the Fat. From the descriptions given in the *Orkneyinga Saga,* it is clear that Thorfinn was far from being handsome. He was described as being big and ugly, with sharp features, black hair and a swarthy complexion. Going on his first raid at the age of fourteen, he soon proved to be a great warrior. But, as the saga says, he could also be greedy, harsh and cruel.

Viking warrior, chessman from Lewis

In the *Orkneyinga Saga* there are many tales of his courage and quick-thinking. On one occasion, while in Orkney, he was taken by surprise and his hall set on fire by his enemies. The doors were guarded by the attackers, and anyone who tried to escape from the blazing building was immediately killed. Quick thinking was essential.

> 'Earl Thorfinn worked out a plan. He broke down part of the woodwork of the house and leaped out there, carrying Ingibiorg, his wife, in his arms. As the night was pitch dark he got away in the smoke unseen. During the night he rowed alone in a boat over to Caithness.'

Unaware that Thorfinn was still alive, the leader of the attackers, Rognvald Brusison, who at that time shared the earldom with Thorfinn, had sailed to Papa Stronsay 'to fetch malt for the Christmas brewing'. Thorfinn followed him there to take his revenge. Rognvald, in his turn, was taken by surprise and trapped in a blazing house. Thorfinn allowed the women and servants to come out. Among them, however, was one man in priest's clothes. He too was allowed to emerge, but Thorfinn's suspicion's were aroused when:

'This man placed his hands on the wall, springing over both it and the ring of men. He came down a great way off and disappeared immediately into the darkness of the night.'

At once Thorfinn realised who it was. Only Rognvald Brusison could have accomplished such a feat. So off went his men in pursuit. Rognvald might have escaped, but he had carried his favourite dog with him. When the dog barked, his hiding-place was revealed, and Thorfinn's men put him to death.

Year after year Thorfinn and his allies waged war in Scotland, the Hebrides and England, winning battles and gaining much plunder. No wonder he came to be called Thorfinn the Mighty. The rulers of Scotland of his time, men like Duncan and Macbeth, were only too aware of the might and power of this northern earl. His conquests included, the saga claims, 'eleven earldoms in Scotland, all the Hebrides and a large part of Ireland'. This is probably an exaggeration, but there is no doubt that he was able to entertain his followers most royally.

'Earl Thorfinn made himself famous by entertaining his own men and many other men of note throughout the winter, so that no one had to go to inns. He provided food and drink at his own expense, in the same way as great men in other countries entertain their followers and guests at Christmas time.'

Swedish Viking head, carved from an elk's horn

In 1048 Earl Thorfinn set off on a pilgrimage to Rome. First he sailed to Norway to make his peace with the king there. Then, after visiting Denmark, he travelled overland through Germany, whose emperor gave him horses to enable him to complete the journey. On reaching the holy city, he was received by the pope and was forgiven for his all-too-many sins. When he returned home, he determined to live in peace.

'He left off making war expeditions, and turned his mind to the government of his land and his people, and to the making of laws.'

Remains of the cathedral built by Earl Thorfinn

By his palace on the Brough of Birsay, which is a tidal island off the mainland of Orkney, he built a fine church. This became a bishop's seat, the first bishopric in the Northern Isles. The photograph above shows the remains of Thorfinn's cathedral. By our standards it is rather small, but the *Orkneyinga Saga* describes it as 'a splendid church'. The aerial photograph below shows that on this small island, the Brough of Birsay, there were a number of Norse buildings of various kinds. The cathedral is in the middle of the cluster. It can be identified by the rounded end, or apse, where the high altar was sited. Traces of a Pictish cemetery have also been found, so it seems that the Norsemen built their church on a site that had long been a holy place. The rectangular buildings, grouped round a courtyard close to the cathedral, are the remains of the bishop's palace.

The Brough of Birsay, Orkney

Archaeologists at work near Thorfinn's cathedral

Nearest to the shore stand the foundations of the earl's palace. One unusual feature was a kind of central heating, which warmed the great hall of the palace. There was also a sauna-type bath-house of a kind that was fairly common in Norse settlements. The photographs on this page show the remains of some of the other buildings. Why do you think there were so many buildings on this tiny island?

It was in 1065 that Earl Thorfinn died, the year before the battles of Stamford Bridge and Hastings. After his death, many of the territories he had conquered were lost. No other earl of Orkney ever matched his achievements.

8. A murder and a pilgrimage

In 1919 an oak coffin, containing human bones, was discovered in the cathedral church of Kirkwall. The skull, as you can see from the photograph on the left, had been damaged by a blow from above. Who was this man, and why had he been killed? Why had his remains been placed within one of the pillars of this church, the largest and most famous in the Northern Isles? For the answers to these questions, we turn now to the *Orkneyinga Saga.*

The story starts about fifty years after the death of Thorfinn. Orkney, after a period of peace, was in a turmoil. Two cousins, Hakon and Magnus, had inherited the earldom, and they had become bitter rivals. To avoid further dispute, Earl Hakon proposed that both earls should meet to arrange a peace treaty. This meeting was to take place in Easter week on a small island called Egilsay. The two earls agreed to bring an equal number of men, and only two ships.

On the day appointed, Magnus, with his two ships, arrived at Egilsay. But when Hakon arrived, he had eight ships and an overwhelming number of warriors. Faced with this treachery, the men with Magnus were prepared to fight. But Magnus refused their offer, saying that they should not sacrifice themselves on his behalf; he would spend his time in prayer, and await his fate.

With Magnus at his mercy, Hakon determined to be rid of his rival. Deciding that his cousin had to die immediately, he asked his standard-bearer to be the executioner, but he angrily refused to carry out this dishonourable act. Hakon then forced his cook, Lifolf, to act as executioner. Lifolf, too, was reluctant, and he began to weep aloud. Then Magnus, his victim, tried to comfort him.

'Weep not, for this is an honourable duty. Don't be afraid, for you do this against your will, and it is not your blame. Stand in front of me, and hew a great wound on my head, for I do not wish to be executed like a thief.'

To think about

1 *Here are two wise sayings from a collection that many Vikings knew by heart. Who remembered the first and who forgot the second?*
'Animals die, families die and we ourselves will die. But, if we leave a good reputation behind us, that will never die.'
'Whenever you open a door, watch out: there may be an enemy waiting behind it.'

To find out

2 *Some of the illustrations in this chapter are of Lewis chessmen. Can you find them and say which pieces they are?*

To do

3 *Draw a cartoon history of Earl Rognvald's life and adventures. Don't forget the stories in chapters 5 and 6.*

4 *Imagine you are a reporter. Give an eye-witness account of either the death of Earl Magnus or of the pilgrimage led by Earl Rognvald. You may like to record your story on tape, with suitable sound effects.*

After crossing himself, Magnus faced his executioner, bowing forward to receive the blow. Lifolf did not delay. He struck with his axe, hewing the 'great wound' that ended the life of Magnus, Earl of Orkney.

If you examine the photograph on page 34, you will see the marks left on the skull by a weapon which crashed down on the victim's head. Had Magnus been executed in the usual way, the blow would have fallen on the back of the head. The skull that was discovered in 1919 must belong to the earl, who met his end in 1117, and who, before he died, prayed for his murderers and forgave them their sins.

This church was built on Egilsay, the island where Magnus died, in about 1137, twenty years after his death

Though Magnus was dead, the story does not end there. His body was taken to Birsay for burial in the church built by his grandfather Thorfinn. As time went on the dead earl came to be regarded as a saint. Miraculous cures were claimed by sick people who had prayed at his grave, and stories were told of a heavenly light that could be seen there.

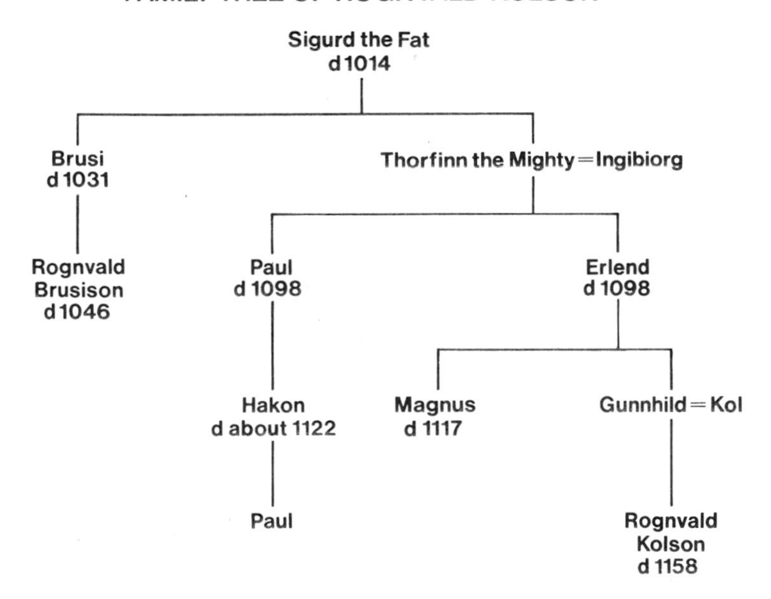

Nearly twenty years later a new figure came on the scene. This was Rognvald Kolson (some of whose adventures have been recounted in earlier chapters). Rognvald, a nephew of the dead Magnus, now claimed his uncle's share of the earldom, and was prepared to fight for it. Hakon was dead, but his son Paul was not going to give way, and he easily defeated Rognvald's first attempt to conquer the islands. Rognvald, forced to retreat to Norway, vowed that, if he were successful when next he tried, he would build a splendid church in memory of his uncle, the holy Magnus.

So Rognvald set out on another attempt to gain the earldom, sailing first to Shetland, where he was made welcome. But he still had to conquer the Orkney islands. To reach Orkney, he had to pass the little isle of Fair Isle, where a beacon could be lit to warn of an attack. To ensure surprise, Rognvald sent a spy to Fair Isle. He managed to soak the beacon with water, so that when Rognvald and his men approached Orkney, no warning had been given. They managed to land without opposition, and there was no fighting, as the Bishop of Orkney arranged a short truce to see if a suitable settlement could be reached.

The coast of Rousay. You can see that Sweyn and his men needed their sleeping-bags to hide them as they approached this open shore.

But the issue was settled in a mysterious way. A young chieftain called Sweyn Asleifson, who had been outlawed by Earl Paul, returned to Orkney when he heard of the troubles there. With a ship-load of men he approached the island of Rousay, where Earl Paul and some attendants happened to be hunting for otters. Sweyn, with most of his men lying low and hidden by their sleeping-bags (which were made of skins), approached the shore. Taken completely by surprise, the earl's bodyguard were all killed and the earl taken prisoner. Sweyn took Earl Paul south to Scotland, but what happened to him there is a mystery. One thing, however, is certain: Earl Paul was never seen again in Orkney, so Rognvald was now the unchallenged ruler of Orkney.

To understand the reason for the quarrel between Earl Paul and Sweyn Asleifson, we have to go back in time to the preceding Yule (or Christmas) feast, which was being held in the earl's hall in Orphir on the Orkney mainland. Sweyn was present, but he had a lot on his mind. A few days previously his father had been surprised by an enemy, and burned to death in his home in Caithness. Then news came of another disaster, Sweyn's brother, with nine of his men, had been drowned on his way to the feast.

The earl was sympathetic: 'Let no-one say anything to annoy Sweyn, as he has troubles enough as it is.' But one of Earl Paul's henchmen, who was an old enemy of Sweyn's, tried to pick a quarrel with him. This was Sweyn Breastrope, a great warrior but a surly and evil character. When he was overheard muttering to himself 'Sweyn will be the death of Sweyn', it was clear that trouble was to be expected. Forewarned, the younger Sweyn decided to strike first. When the earl and his party left the hall to attend midnight mass at an adjacent church, Sweyn Asleifson waited behind, lurking in the shadows. As the earl's henchman made his way outside, his young namesake struck him on the forehead with an axe. Then, on a horse provided by friends, Sweyn Asleifson galloped away from the earl's hall.

Angry at Sweyn's conduct, Earl Paul declared him an outlaw. But this meant that the earl had made an enemy, and, as we have seen, Sweyn was the most dangerous enemy of them all.

Sweyn Breastrope may have looked like this surly Viking warrior—one of the chessmen from Lewis

Visitors to Orkney today can see the foundations of the earl's hall in Orphir where 'Sweyn was the death of Sweyn'. Close to it are the remains of the church where, as the saga describes, the Yule guests of Earl Paul went to hear mass. Being round, it was an unusual church, although hardly so 'magnificent' as is claimed in the saga. How can you tell from the picture that it was not a very large building?

A Norse bishop—one of the Lewis chessmen

Truly magnificent, as you can see, was the church built by Earl Rognvald, in thanksgiving for his success. Started in 1137, the work of construction was soon under way with Earl Rognvald's father, Kol, in charge. Probably the Bishop of Orkney, William the Old, who was a scholar of Paris and a widely travelled man, was also involved in its planning. Although it took several hundred years before it was completed, it stands today as a monument not only to Magnus, Kol and Rognvald, but also to the countless men, the humble and forgotten, who helped to build it.

Saint Magnus Cathedral, Kirkwall. This old print shows the massive pillars and high ceiling inside the church.

Although his reign was troubled, Earl Rognvald proved to be a popular and successful ruler. A real all-rounder, he could boast of a variety of talents, including archery, rowing, skiing, making runes, playing the harp and doing practical work with his hands. There were two other skills that Rognvald possessed.

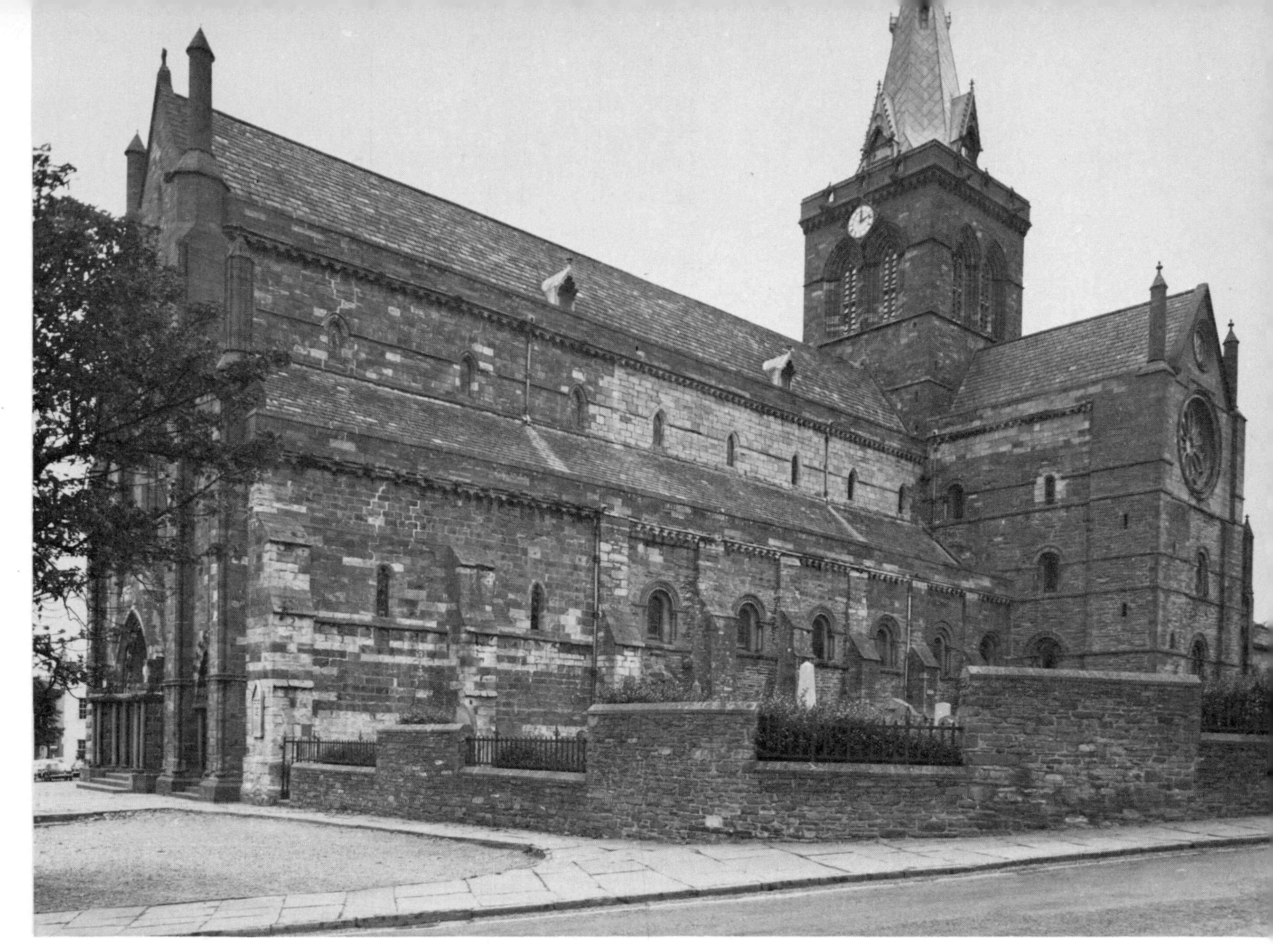

Saint Magnus Cathedral today

One was his ability to win at the gaming-board. We don't know for sure how the game was played, but a squared-off board or slate was used. On the right you can see a slate used in these games, one of several found at Jarlshof. As to his other skill, you may recall reading about it earlier. If you turn back to page 23, you can refresh your memory about it.

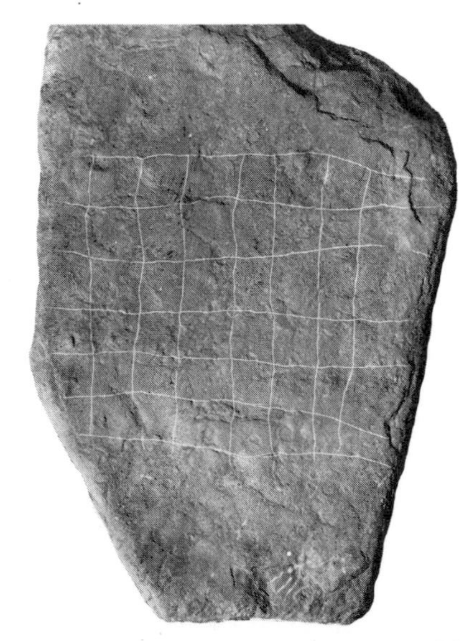

In chapter 5, we read of a party of Norsemen who went on a journey to the Holy Land with Earl Rognvald as one of the leaders. Their voyage to Jerusalem was marked by a series of adventures, which included storming a castle in Spain and capturing, near Sardinia, a Saracen treasure ship. As the Holy Land was then enjoying a period of peace, there was no problem in visiting all the holy places. When the Norsemen reached the River Jordan, Earl Rognvald and a companion, Sigmund Fish-hook, swam across and tied some shrubs into knots. This they did as a challenge to the stay-at-homes to come and untie them.

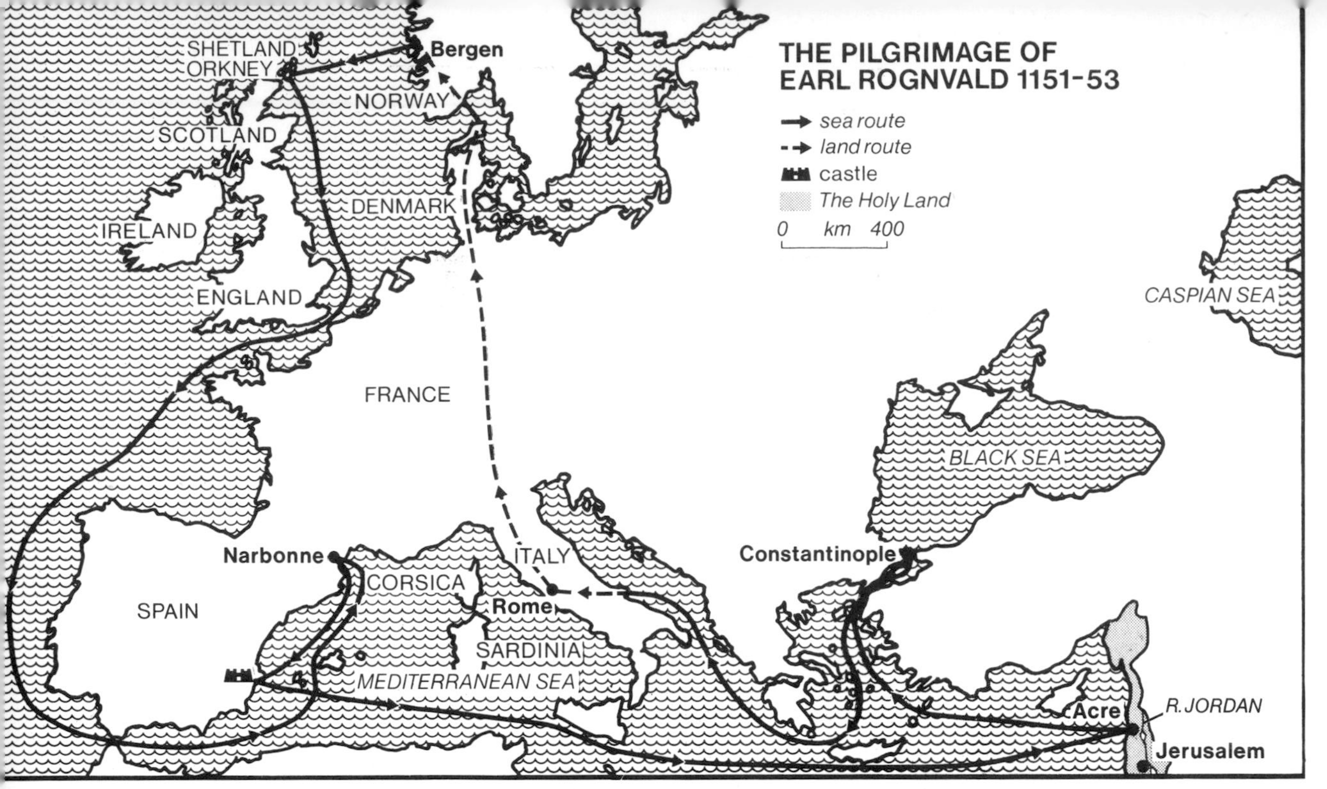

On their return journey those happy-go-lucky pilgrims visited Constantinople, whose Emperor tried to entice them to join his bodyguard. Refusing this offer, they sailed to Italy, and, after visiting Rome, rode towards home, taking the overland route. Then they visited Norway, before returning to Orkney in 1153. This jaunt, which lasted two and a half years, became very famous. The *Orkneyinga Saga* says:

> 'All those who went on this journey were considered greater men afterwards than before.'

One man who did not go on this journey was Sweyn Asleifson, but he led an adventurous enough life at any rate. His numerous raids and other exploits brought him great wealth. It was his practice to spend the winter on the small island of Gairsay off the mainland of Orkney. To provide for his bodyguard, which numbered eighty men, he had built the largest drinking-hall in all the islands. In the spring he then busied himself with farm work, sowing the seed-corn and doing a great part of the work himself. When this work was finished, he sailed off on what he called his spring-viking cruise, plundering in the Hebrides, Ireland and elsewhere. Returning home after midsummer, he stayed at home till the harvest was in. Then, in the words of the *Orkneyinga Saga*:

> 'He went raiding again, and did not return till one month of winter had passed. This he called his autumn-viking cruise.'

During the winter months, the boats would have been drawn into shelters or *nousts,* which gave protection from the winter gales. As the photograph on the right shows, such nousts are still common in the Northern Isles.

On one of his spring-viking raids, Sweyn, with five large rowing ships, sailed first to the Hebrides, where the inhabitants were so afraid of him that they hid all their valuables in the ground or under loose stones. Finding little booty in the Isle of Man, he next made for Ireland. Near Dublin he captured two English merchant-ships, laden with fine cloth and other merchandise. The English seamen, who gave little resistance, were spared and allowed to keep their ships, but the Vikings 'took every penny in the vessels, leaving to the Englishmen only what they stood in, and a small quantity of food.' When Sweyn's longships returned home, they had the fine cloth sewed on to the sails to show off the value of their loot.

This carved wooden animal-head probably decorated a chair belonging to a Norse chieftain

In 1171 Sweyn set off on what was to be his last voyage. His force was a strong one, no fewer than seven longships. Reaching Ireland, he took the inhabitants of Dublin by surprise and captured the city. After agreeing to the Orcadians' terms, the city leaders broke their word and prepared an ambush. Off their guard, Sweyn and his men walked into the trap. In the fight that followed Sweyn was killed. So died the last and the most famous of the Orkney raiders. The *Orkneyinga Saga* concludes:

> 'Here is the end of the story of Sweyn. And it has been said that he was the greatest man of his rank in the western lands, either in old times or at the present day.'

 **To think about**

1 What do you think might have happened to Hakon's own ship? Do you think that it might have been buried like the Gokstad and Oseberg ships shown on pages 5 and 12?

2 Why, in your opinion, did Magnus Bareleg spare Iona in 1098? Why did he not sack the monastery as the first raiders did in 795?

 **To find out**

3 Discover what you can about the Scottish kings mentioned in this chapter.

4 Find out more about the history of the Isle of Man. When did it cease to be part of the Scottish kingdom?

 **To do**

5 Draw a picture in colour of Hakon's flagship.

6 Make a frieze or series of cartoons telling the story of the Norse in Scotland from the days of Harald Finehair (see page 10) to 1468.

9. The decline of Norse power

In the course of time the kings of Scotland began to extend their powers and territories. In the north, for instance, King William the Lion (1165-1214) made determined efforts to control Ross, Sutherland and Caithness.

The Western Isles proved a much more difficult task, for in that region there were many men seeking power, including, as well as native rulers, the earls of Orkney and the Norse kings of Man and of Dublin. Occasionally, too, a king of Norway would arrive, leading an expedition to assert his claim as overlord.

In 1098 Magnus Bareleg, King of Norway, led such an expedition. Looting and burning, he left in his wake a trail of death and devastation. Only one island was spared, the holy island of Iona. You can see part of the island in the picture below. Magnus kept his men from damaging the little church of St Columba. Instead, he offered peace and safety to all who lived on the island.

In the *Heimskringla,* the saga of the Norse kings, we learn of the treaty made by the kings of Norway and of Scotland. According to the saga, King Magnus was to possess all the western islands between which and the mainland he could pass in a ship with a rudder. But Magnus was not content to have just the islands. He also wanted to claim the peninsula of Kintyre. This he accomplished by having his men drag a skiff across the isthmus at its narrowest point. In this small boat, we are told, sat the Norse king, holding the helm. Thus Magnus Bareleg laid his claim to the 'island' of Kintyre. The rudder he held would have been like this steering oar, shown in a sketch from Jarlshof. Historians cannot say whether this story is true or false. It may be a legend, but there is no doubt that an adventurer like Magnus Bareleg was just the kind of man to invent such a plan.

Later Scottish rulers resumed the struggle against the Norsemen. During the reign of Alexander II (1214-1249), Argyll, including Kintyre, returned to Scottish control. The Norse threat was not easily removed, however, as the Scottish lords of Bute found to their cost. When this island in the Firth of Clyde was recovered from the Norse around 1200, a fine stone castle was built at Rothesay to protect it.

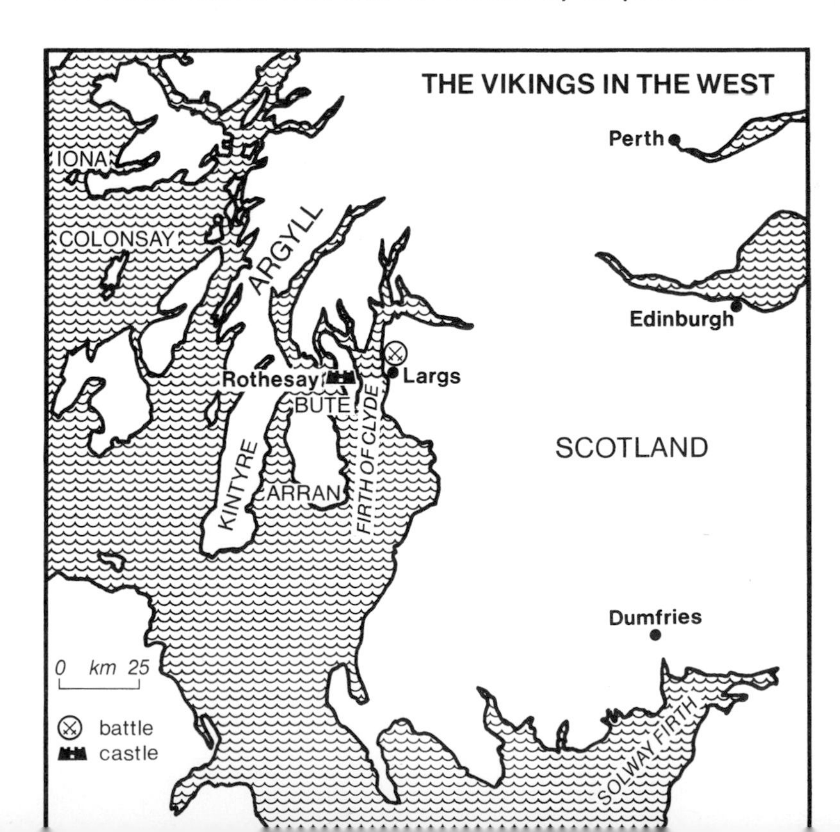

Rothesay castle ruins. Can you see the moat?

But in 1230 Norse raiders returned to the island of Bute, and laid siege to the castle. Finding that the stone was soft, the Norsemen cut into the outer wall with their axes. Although the defenders poured pitch (boiling tar) over them, they so weakened the wall that a section of it collapsed, enabling the attackers to enter and take the castle.

Later Scottish kings made attempts to win back all of the Western Isles. Both Alexander II and Alexander III even offered to purchase the islands. Eventually, in 1263, one of the greatest of all the Norwegian kings, Hakon IV, decided that a show of strength was needed. Leading a mighty fleet of some 150 ships, he sailed down the west coast of Scotland before anchoring in the Firth of Clyde, off Arran.

Playing for time, Alexander III tried to negotiate with the Norsemen. Then a great storm struck the Norse fleet, driving some of their ships onto the shore at Largs. When a Norse force landed to salvage some cargo, they were attacked by the Scots. The fight on the beach, among the stranded ships, was a fierce one. We cannot be sure who won this so-called battle of Largs—both sides were later to claim the victory. As the Norsemen did not attempt to hold their ground, the Scots probably gained the advantage.

Two photographs of the Battle of Largs monument, built in 1912. On the left you can see the high tower, designed to look like an old Irish or Celtic tower. On the right is the doorway, carved in Celtic style.

Once the crippled Norse fleet had left for home, the way was open for the Scots to invade the islands of the west. Recognising that it was too much trouble to hold on to such distant territories, Hakon's successor agreed to sell them. By a treaty signed at Perth in 1266, the Hebrides (and the Isle of Man too) were transferred to Scottish control.

What, you may wonder, had happened to Hakon the Great? When, after the fight at Largs, the remnants of the Norse fleet reached Orkney, Hakon was a sick man. Deciding to spend the winter in Orkney, he took up residence in the bishop's palace at Kirkwall. A visit to the shrine of St Magnus in the cathedral nearby brought no cure. Confined to bed, the king had holy books read to him. When he grew too feeble to follow the Latin, he asked for Norse works to be read instead. First, we are told, he listened to the lives of the saints; then to the sagas which told of the deeds of his ancestors. The last to be read was the saga of his grandfather, King Sverre:

> 'Near midnight Sverre's saga was finished, and just as midnight was past Almighty God called King Hakon from this world's life.'

For the time being Hakon was laid to rest in the cathedral at Kirkwall. Then in the spring a mighty longship, with dragon-head and tail all covered in gold, left Scapa Flow for Bergen. It was the king's own flagship, bearing back to Norway the remains of King Hakon, the last of the great sea-kings.

An old view of the ruins of the bishop's palace, Kirkwall, where King Hakon died. In the background is the cathedral where his body was laid before it was taken back to Norway.

Though the Western Isles had been lost, Orkney and Shetland still owed allegiance to the kings of Norway. But the golden age of the earldom was over. Rognvald, who died in 1158, was the last of the Norse earls to make a great name for himself. His successor lost control of Shetland, which came directly under the rule of the kings of Norway. In Caithness, too, the Norse had lost ground. And from 1231 the earldom of Orkney was held by men who were of Scottish origin. Scottish influence was thus bound to extend.

Ironically, as the men of Orkney turned to peaceful pursuits, they in their turn suffered from raids and pirate attacks. In 1461 the bishop of Orkney wrote a letter to the king complaining that:

> 'Raiders from the Hebrides and Ireland invaded the earldom of Orkney in great numbers, with their fleets and boats in warlike manner. They have burned your lands, towns, houses and buildings to the ground, and put to the sword men, women, and children. Everything they could lift they have stolen—including animals, goods, jewels, and money.'

For the descendants of the Vikings, the wheel had come full circle.

The end came when King Christian I, who was ruler of both Denmark and Norway, agreed to marry his daughter Margaret to James III of Scotland. A large sum of money was to be paid as Margaret's dowry. As Christian could not raise the whole sum, first Orkney in 1468 and then Shetland in the following year were transferred to Scotland as pledges for the remainder. In effect, the islands were pawned. As no more cash was paid, the islands remained in Scottish hands.

When the Vikings were at the peak of their power, the Northern Isles were of great strategic importance. But once the longships had departed from the oceans, these isles returned to their former obscurity. Then, some 600 years after the death of Hakon, mighty fleets once again sailed in these northern waters. When Britain went to war against Germany in 1914, Scapa Flow in Orkney, where Hakon's longships had anchored in 1263, became the base for the British Grand Fleet. In 1914 and again in 1939, when the Second World War broke out, the islands of Orkney once more loomed large in the pages of history.

Today both Orkney and Shetland feature as important centres for the developing North Sea oil industry. Yet again these islands of the north are a cross-roads and a focus of attention.

German warship in Scapa Flow at the end of the First World War, 1919

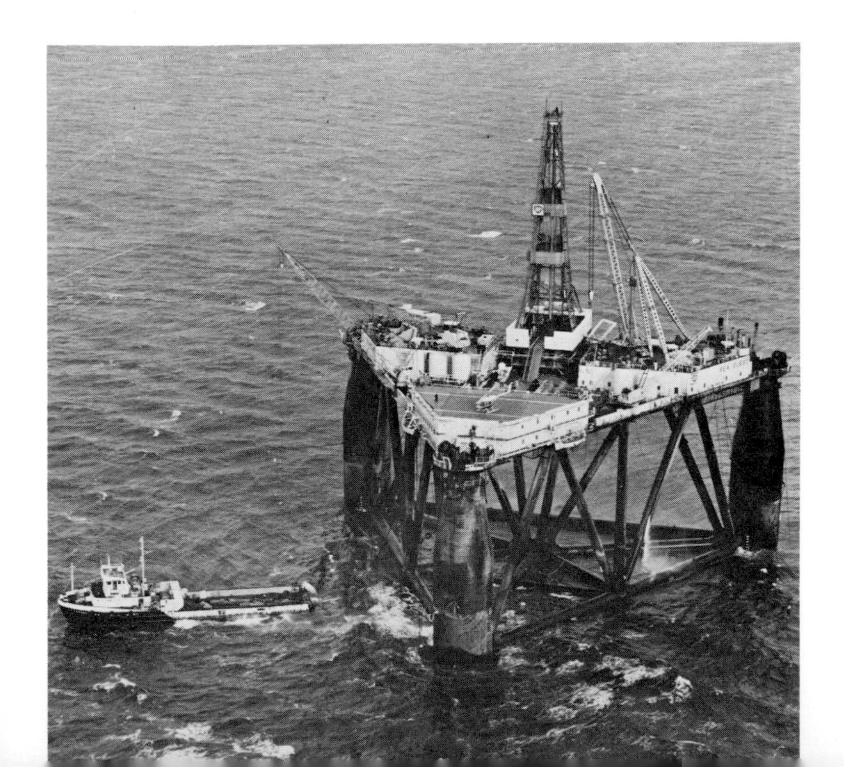

The oil-rig Sea-Quest in the North Sea

Index